Macmillan/McGraw-Hill READING

Contributors

The Princeton Review, Time Magazine, Accelerated Reader

The Princeton Review is not
affiliated with Princeton
University or ETS.

Students with print disabilities may be eligible to obtain an accessible, audio
version of the pupil edition of this textbook. Please call Recording for the Blind &
Dyslexic at 1-800-221-4792 for complete information.

Macmillan/McGraw-Hill

A Division of The **McGraw·Hill** Companies

Published by Macmillan/McGraw-Hill, a division of The McGraw-Hill Companies, Inc., Two Penn Plaza, NY, NY 10121

Printed in the United States of America

ISBN 0-02-188564-8/1, Bk.4

2 3 4 5 6 7 8 9 027/043 04 03 02

Macmillan/McGraw-Hill READING

Authors

James Flood

Jan E. Hasbrouck

James V. Hoffman

Diane Lapp

Donna Lubcker

Angela Shelf Medearis

Scott Paris

Steven Stahl

Josefina Villamil Tinajero

Karen D. Wood

Macmillan
McGraw-Hill

New York   Farmington

Let's Find Out

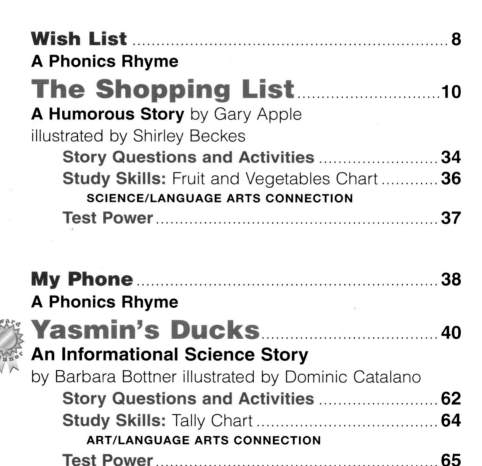

Let's Find Out

To the Top

We're climbing and climbing
The trail is so high
that I think we'll be climbing
right up to the sky.
I want it to end
and my poor feet to stop.
Oh, when will we reach
the mountaintop?

by Sandra Liatsos

Wish List

I made a silly shopping list
Of things I want to get:
Five limes, a kite, a bike,
Four plums (they have to be ripe),
A snake that slides, and skates that shine.

Do you think I could get all this
With a dime?

Meet Gary Apple

When Gary Apple was a little boy, he liked to write funny stories. Now that he is grown up, he still likes to write funny stories. Today, he writes funny books, plays, and TV shows.

Meet Shirley Beckes

Shirley Beckes is an illustrator of children's books, puzzles, and games. She owns her own design studio in Wisconsin.

The Shopping List

by Gary Apple

illustrated by Shirley Beckes

One day Mike went to his dad's
store with a list.

Dad was always glad to see Mike.

"Hi, there, Mike!" said Dad with a grin.

"Hi!" said Mike. "Mom sent me to get some things."

Mike checked his list. "Let's see," he said.
"Mom wants me to get jam and rice.
She needs five ripe plums, too."

Dad got the rice, the jam, and the five ripe plums.

"Thanks a lot!" said Mike.

Mike packed them in a big bag.

"There was something else I had to get," said Mike.

"What is it?" asked Dad.

"I didn't write it down," said Mike. "I can't remember now."

"I can help you," said Dad. "Did Mom
ask for fresh fish?"

"No, it was not fish," said Mike.

"Well, did Mom want you to get
some grapes?" asked Dad.
"No, she didn't ask for grapes," said Mike.

18

"Is it punch? Is it milk? Is it something to drink?"
asked Dad.

"No. It was not something to drink," said Mike.

Just then, Miss Lin came in.

"What's going on?" she asked.

"Mike can't remember what he came
to get," said Dad.

"Maybe I can help," said Miss Lin. "Does it come in a big box?"

"Does it come in a small sack?" asked Dad.

"Does it come in tin cans or glass jars?"
asked Miss Lin.
But Mike still could not remember.

Then Fran and Ann Gomez came in.
Soon, they were trying to help, too.

"What color is it?" asked Fran.
"Is it red, blue, white, or black?" asked Ann.

Then Miss Lin jumped in. "Is it
carrots, muffins, or bread?"
"No, no, and no!" said Mike.

Then together, Fran, Ann, Dad,
and Miss Lin spoke. "Is it this or that?
Is it that or this? Do you cut it?
Do you chop it?"

"I know!" said Miss Lin. "You were sent to get dog food!"

"Who needs that?" asked Mike.

"We do not have a dog!"

Dad looked in every row.

Miss Lin looked on every shelf.

Fran looked up and down.

Ann looked down and up!

After they had looked everywhere,
Miss Lin said, "I give up!"
"And we give up, too!" said Ann and Fran.

"Think, Mike, think!" said Dad. "What were you sent to get?"
Mike said, "Let me think."

Mike looked at the messy store.

Then Mike looked at Dad.

A wide smile filled Mike's face.

"Mom wanted me to get…!" he said.

"What is it?" yelled Miss Lin.

"Tell us!" yelled Fran and Ann.

Mike smiled and said, "Mom asked me
to get YOU, Dad. It's time for supper!"

Story Questions & Activities

1. What foods were on Mike's list?

2. What happened to Dad's store?

3. Why do you think Mike forgot?

4. Pretend you are Mike and tell about your day.

5. Tell how Meg from "Splash!" also forgot something.

Draw Two Kinds of Fruit

Choose two fruits from the story.
Draw a picture of each one.
Write how they are alike.

Both are red.

Play a Memory Game

Play in a group.
One person begins:

"I went to the store to buy soap."

The next person says:

"I went to the store to buy soap and bananas."

Keep playing.
See how many items you remember.

Find Out More

Find out about one food that is good for you.
Tell about the food and how it helps you.

Fruit or Vegetable?

Fruits	Vegetables
peach	carrot
plum	string beans
cherry	

Look at the Chart

1 Which are listed as fruits?

2 Name an orange vegetable.

Mike's Pet

Mike has a fish.

It lives in a fish tank.

Mike feeds his fish every day.

The food sits on top of the water.

The fish swims to the top to eat the food.

Then, it swims back down to the bottom.

Why does the fish swim to the top?

○ To say hello to Mike

○ To eat the food

Ask yourself: "What does the story tell me?"

My Phone

I hope and hope to get a phone,
One that is mine and mine alone.
I hope and hope to get a phone,
A rose one with a quack-quack tone.

I will not be sad, you see,
With a phone that is just for me!

Meet Barbara Bottner

When Barbara Bottner was a young woman, she was an actress. When she was touring with a group of actors, she broke her leg. While she was getting better, Bottner realized how much she loved to draw. She began to illustrate children's books. Soon she was writing stories to go along with her pictures. Now Bottner loves to write and she spends most of her time writing.

Meet Dominic Catalano

Dominic Catalano has illustrated several children's books. He is also a musician. Catalano owns a design studio.

Yasmin's Ducks

written by Barbara Bottner

illustrated by Dominic Catalano

"These are the best ducks I have
ever made!" said Yasmin.
"I can just see them in the lake.
They swim around and quack.
Quack, quack, quack," said Yasmin.

"Ducks, ducks, ducks!" said Ben.
"I like your ducks."

"Look, Mom, do you like my ducks?" asked Yasmin.

"Yes, they are fine ducks," she said.

"I will take them to class. It's show-and-tell day," said Yasmin.

Miss Rome's class held up their work.

Tim made pictures of fish with fins.
"I like to make my fish with lots of colors,"
said Tim. "I have five blue and white fish
at home. I hope to buy a red fish."

Kate made fire trucks with big hoses.
"I like to make big, red fire trucks. My dad
is a fireman. He is very brave," said Kate.

Mack said, "I like to make rocket ships.
They can go around the globe and back!"

Yasmin held up her ducks. "I like ducks the best," she said. "I want to make ducks with wings that shine! I want to make ducks that swim and quack!"

"Why do you like to make ducks?"
Tim, Kate, and Mack asked.

"Well, I just read a good book on ducks.
I found out a lot about them," said Yasmin.

"What did you learn?" Kate asked.

"Did you know that ducks don't get wet?" Yasmin asked.

"Wow," Yasmin's pals said.

"It's no joke," Yasmin added.

"How come they don't get wet?" Kate asked.

"A duck has oil next to its tail," said
Yasmin. "It wipes the oil all around its
feathers. The duck's feathers don't get wet
because water and oil don't mix. The water
rolls off its back," Yasmin said.

"That's cool," Mack said.

"Let's all go to my house after school,"
Yasmin said. "I'll show you how ducks
don't get wet."

When they got home, Yasmin got out her
book on ducks. "We need two bags and
salad oil," said Yasmin.

"First, you put the oil on one lunch bag.
Then you put some water on both bags,"
said Yasmin.

"Look at that!" Tim said.

"That bag isn't wet," Kate said.

"The water drips off!" Tim said.

"Water and oil really don't mix,"
Mack said.

"What about this? Did you know that ducks can dive to the bottom of very deep lakes?" Yasmin asked.

"And they don't get wet!" Yasmin's pals said.

"Nope! They don't," Yasmin said.

"Did you know that ducks fly south in the fall?" asked Yasmin.

"When it's fall, the ducks can't get plants to eat because the lake is cold. They go south where they can eat."

"They fly in a big flock," said Mack.
"I saw them last fall."

"I think I like ducks, too," Tim said.

"Me, too. I wish I didn't have to go home now," said Kate.

"It's raining out," Yasmin said.

"Too bad we're not ducks!" Tim said.
"Then we would not get wet!"

Yasmin and her pals smiled.
"Quack, quack, quack, quack!"

1 What do ducks do in the fall?

2 Why does Yasmin need two bags and salad oil?

3 Why don't the children want to go home?

4 What did you learn from this story?

5 Is "What Bug Is It?" like this story?

Write About the Experiment

Yasmin puts oil on one bag.

Then she puts water on both bags.

Write what happens to each bag.

The bag with the oil is not wet.

Play Duck, Duck, Goose

Sit in a circle.

Think of names of birds.

Play Duck, Duck, Goose.

Play again and use other bird names.

Have fun!

Find Out More

Find out about another water bird.

How is it like a duck?

How is it different from a duck?

A Class Vote

This chart shows what some children draw.

Count the lines.

See how many children draw each thing.

What Do You Like to Draw?	
ducks	||||
fish	||
fire trucks	⊬⊬⊬ ⊬⊬⊬
jets	⊬⊬⊬
hats	||||

Look at the Chart

1 How many children like to draw jets?

2 Which thing do the most children like to draw?

64

Jasmin and Her Kite

Jasmin takes her kite outside.

She finds a place with no trees.

She unrolls her kite string.

She holds her kite up high.

The wind picks up the kite.

The kite begins to fly.

Soon it is high in the sky.

Why does Jasmin's kite fly?

○ The wind picks it up.

○ There are no trees.

Ask yourself the question in your own words.

Duke the Ant

Duke the ant is quite a dude.

He is very polite and never rude.

Duke the ant is small and cute.

He plays music on his new flute.

Duke the ant is always in tune!

He gave a concert just last June.

Duke can make a tone that's pure.

Duke the bug is cool, for sure!

Meet Ellen Dreyer

Ellen Dreyer has always loved writing. She has written many children's books. She gets her ideas from talking with children. Dreyer also teaches creative writing to children. She says it is important for writers to keep a notebook and write down what they see and hear.

Meet Tim Raglin

Tim Raglin illustrates children's books, magazines, and advertisements. He spent a lot of time drawing as a boy, and later went to art school. Raglin likes to draw animals in human situations. He says, "If you like to draw, just keep practicing."

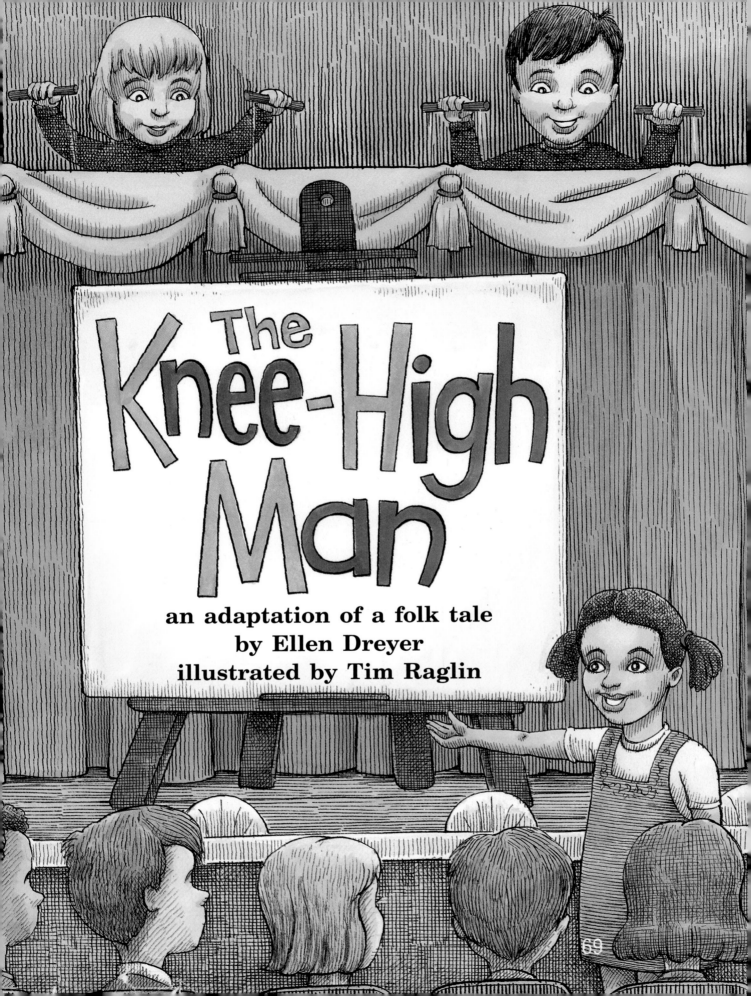

The Knee-High Man

an adaptation of a folk tale
by Ellen Dreyer
illustrated by Tim Raglin

The Players:

June
A Storyteller

Bob Bull

Sam
The Knee-High
Man

Kate Owl

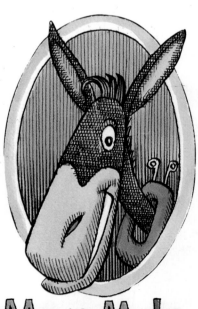

Max Mule

June: Some folks grow big. Some folks stay small. That's a rule of life. But Sam, the Knee-High Man, wanted to be big. He just had to find out how to do it.

71

Sam: Max Mule is sure to know how I can get big like him. He will tell me how to grow.

Max: What's up, Sam?

Sam: Max, you are so big! The bugs carry
rope to get down from your back.
How can I get big like you?

Max: This is what you do. Pick lots of corn cobs. Clean them, eat them, and then run ten miles. Try that, Sam. In time, you will be big, just like me.

Sam: Thanks, Max. I sure will try.

June: So Sam cleaned and then chomped on ten corn cobs. He ran ten miles, too. When he was done, his tummy hurt and his legs hurt. But he did not grow one inch. He just got mad, as mad as can be.

Sam: What have I done? I ate that much.
I ran that far. And I am still small!

June: But Sam did not give up. No, not Sam, the Knee-High Man.

Sam: Bob Bull is the biggest one I know.
He is sure to know how I can get big
like him. I will go see him. He will
tell me what to do.

Sam: Bob Bull, you are so big. Frogs think
your horns are tree branches. How
can I get big like you?

Bob: Well, Sam, this is what you do. Eat a
lot of fine grass and yell and grunt a
lot. Try that, Sam. In time, you will
be a big old brute, just like me.

June: Sam ate a peck of grass. He yelled and grunted till the sun set. When he was done, his tummy hurt and his throat hurt. But he did not grow one inch!

Sam: What bad, bad luck! I ate that grass.
I yelled and grunted. And I am still
small!

June: But Sam did not give up. No, not Sam, the Knee-High Man. He went to see Kate Owl.

Sam: Kate Owl is very wise. She will tell
me how I can get bigger, for sure.

Sam: Kate, you are wise. Tell me how I can get bigger. I have been trying my best.

Kate: Why do you want to be big, Sam?

Sam: If I am big, then I can win any fight.

Kate: Who has picked a fight with you?

Sam: No one.

Kate: Then you do not have to fight.
And you do not have to be big.

Sam: But if I am big, I can see far away.
I can see far, just like you.

Kate: Can't you go up a tree to look far away?

Sam: Sure I can!

Kate: You see, Sam. You do not have to
be bigger. You are just fine the way
you are.

Sam: I think you are right, Kate.
Because if I were any bigger, I would
not be me. I would not be Sam,
the Knee-High Man!

Story Questions & Activities

1 What did Bob tell Sam to do?

2 Why is Sam called the Knee-High Man?

3 How did Kate help Sam?

4 Tell what you think Sam learned.

5 How is a play different from a story?

Draw Sam and Bob

Sam and Bob Bull are friends.
Write how they are the same.
Write how they are different.

Sam is small. Bob is big.

Add to the Play

Work with your class.

Add two more animals to the play.

Make up things for them to say.

Then read the play aloud.

Find Out More

"The Knee-High Man" is a folktale.

It teaches a lesson.

Find another folktale that teaches
a lesson.

Who Said What? Chart

This chart shows what the animals said to Sam.

	Mule	eat corn run ten miles
	Bull	eat grass yell and grunt
	Owl	don't do anything

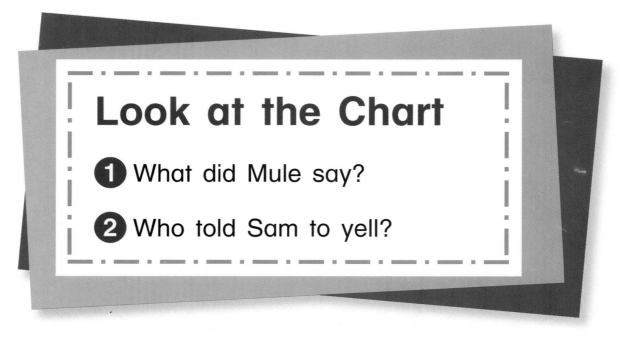

Look at the Chart

1 What did Mule say?

2 Who told Sam to yell?

94

What Is Polly Doing?

Polly put her toes out.

Polly put her legs out.

Polly put her fingers out.

Polly put her arms out.

Polly put her whole self out of bed.

The air was too cold.

So, Polly climbed back into her

warm bed.

Why did Polly climb back into her bed?

○ The air was too cold.

○ She was sleepy.

Think about what the story tells you.

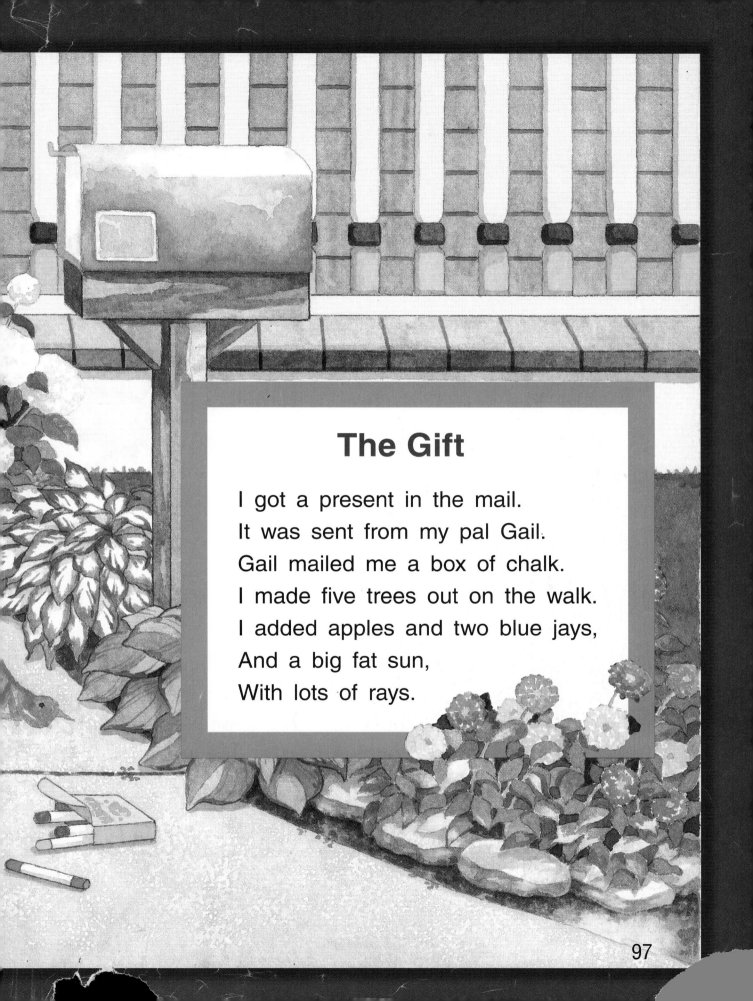

The Gift

I got a present in the mail.
It was sent from my pal Gail.
Gail mailed me a box of chalk.
I made five trees out on the walk.
I added apples and two blue jays,
And a big fat sun,
With lots of rays.

Meet Mary Pope Osborne

When Mary Pope Osborne was little, she lived with her family on different Army bases in the southern United States. When she grew up, she lived in Europe and then traveled across Asia. Her travel experiences gave Osborne ideas to write about when she first started writing.

Meet Michael Steirnagle

Michael Steirnagle has illustrated children's books as well as advertisements. He often uses his two children, Matthew and Stacy, and his dog, Ralph, in his pictures.

Johnny Appleseed

by Mary Pope Osborne

illustrated by Michael Steirnagle

His name was John Chapman.
But he was called Johnny Appleseed.
This is his tale.

He dressed in rags and old sacks.
He had no shoes. A tin pot was his hat.

Johnny knew a lot about plants and how to grow them. He had lots of apple seeds.

One day, he packed his seeds and left
home. He had a plan. He wanted to help
the people who were going west. He
wanted to help them plant apple trees.

He sailed down the river on a raft. "Quick! Plant my apple seeds!" he said to those who were on the banks.

"They will give you pretty, pink buds in May! In the fall, you can make pies and jam!"

As Johnny went west, he passed women in sun hats and men with mules. "Take them and plant them!" he said. And he gave them seeds.

"Where is your home?" they asked him.
He just smiled and went on his way.

In rain and hail, mist and fog, he kept
on. He stayed in sheds with hens and
chicks. He camped in caves with bats.

But he was not sad.
He always had a big smile.
"What a pretty day this is,"
he would say. "Life is very good!"

Some days, he stopped to dig holes and dropped in the seeds. But some days, he just flung them to the wind.

"Do not take them," he would tell the blue jays. "Wait for the trees to grow. As they get bigger, you can live in their branches."

Johnny was a good man.
One time, he mended a quail's wing.
Then he saved a gray wolf from a trap.

One day, he found an old horse.
He fed him and gave him a bath.

Now with his pets, he went to place after place. He visited mills and shops.

"I bring little seeds to grow into big trees!" he said with a big smile. His eyes flashed with light as he explained how to plant them.

Some people did not trust Johnny.
He did not live the way they did.
But most people liked him.
They would ask him into their homes.

He would tell them about his trip west.
They would give him some ham and
cake. Then he would rest.

When the sun came up, he was on
his way. He waved and flung his seeds
to the wind.

When Johnny died, he was missed a lot. But his trees got bigger and bigger. He had given a gift that would live on.

Story Questions & Activities

1 Where did Johnny go?

2 How did Johnny help people?

3 Why did Johnny always smile?

4 Tell about Johnny's life in your own words.

5 What other book have you read about a real person?

Make a Poster

Think about how Johnny's seeds change the land.

Draw the land before his visit.

Then draw the land after his visit.

Label the drawings **Before** and **After**.

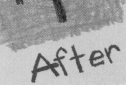

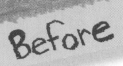

Have an Apple Party!

There are many kinds of apples.
Bring in your favorite kind of apple.
Look at all the apples.
Taste them.
Talk about how they are alike
and different.

Find Out More

Find out about another good American.
Tell what the person did for our country.

Apple Tree Chart

This chart tells how an apple tree grows.

Plant the Seed

Water the Seed

Let It Grow

Pick Apples

Look at the Chart

1 What do you do first to grow an apple tree?

2 What helps the apple tree grow?

122

A Trip to the Barn

It was early in the evening.

Farmer Joe wanted corn for dinner.

He had put the corn in the big red barn.

Farmer Joe put on his boots and walked
out to the barn.

He picked out three ears of corn.

"One, two, three," Farmer Joe counted.

"I can't wait to eat dinner," he said happily.

Then, Farmer Joe took the corn
back to the house.

What will Farmer
Joe do with the corn?

○ Eat it

○ Feed it to the pigs

Read the
story again to
help answer the
question.

Fire Pup

I'm a little fire pup. My name is Spot.
You can ask for me when things get
   very hot.

If you see a fire and if you need
   a water hose,
I'll use my fast fire truck and bring you
   one of those.

Is there a trail of smoke or a bit
   of flame?
Anytime day or night, just yell out
   my name!

TIME FOR KIDS
SPECIAL REPORT

Ring! Ring! Ring! Put Out the Fire!

How do firefighters do their work? They must ride in a big, red fire truck to get to the fire. The big, red fire truck has lots of things that are used to put out fires. The ladder helps the firefighter get to the hot flames. The engine pumps water through the long fire hose. The fire hose sprays it on the fire.

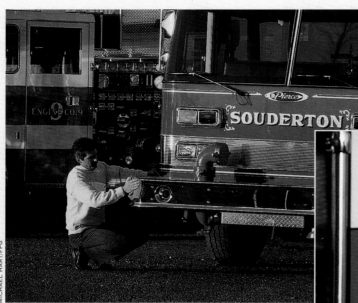
MICHAEL HART/FPG

DOROTHY LITTELL GRECO/STOCK BOSTON

There is always work that has to be done. The fire trucks have to be clean and ready to go. The firefighters have masks to stay safe and keep out smoke and fumes.

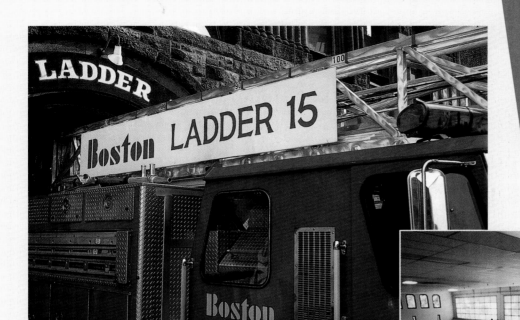

Ring! Ring! Ring! Ring! Ring! The fire bell rings, and the firefighters run! They slide down the long pole and put on fire gear. They rush, rush, rush to put out the fire. They can put out the biggest fires. They are very fast! Don't you think they are brave? Would you want to put out big fires one day?

A story from the editors of *TIME FOR KIDS*.

1. What pumps water through the fire hose?

2. How can you tell if a fire truck is going to a fire?

3. Why must firefighters be strong?

4. Tell about the work a firefighter does.

5. What are some differences between the work of a firefighter and the work of a vet?

Compare Two Jobs

Think about a firefighter and a nurse. How are their jobs the same?

Make a Fire Safety Badge

Make yourself a fire safety badge.
Color it and cut it out.
Wear it on your shirt.

I know how to keep safe from fire.

I know how to keep safe from fire.

I know how to keep safe from fire.

Find Out More

Find out the best way to exit from school and your home in case of a fire.

Vote and Tally

Children voted on what they want to be when they grow up. This tally shows their votes.

When I Grow Up

Job	Number of children
firefighter	||||
baker	||
vet	||||
teacher	卌|

Look at the Tally

1 How many children want to be vets?

2 Which job did the most children want to do?

The Fireplace

The man came in from outside.

He shook the snow off his boots.

He had a bundle of wood in his arms.

He put some wood on the fire.

Then, he put the fire screen in front.

The fire in the fireplace was warm.

It warmed the man's toes.

The man sat down in his chair.

He rocked forward and backward.

His cat came and sat on his lap.

Then, they took a little nap together.

What time of year is it in this story?

○ Summer

○ Winter

Read both answer choices. Which one fits the story?

Who Lived in a Shoe?

You know that old woman
   Who lived in a shoe?
She had so many children
   She didn't know what to do?

I think if she lived in
   A little shoe-house
That little old lady was
   Surely a mouse!

by Beatrix Potter

135

Reading to Find Answers

Asking questions and looking up answers is called research. We can look for answers in different places.

> Where do tigers live?
> What do tigers eat?

Look It Up

Suppose you want to find out about tigers. Where can you look?

- You can look in a dictionary.
- You can look in books at the library.
- You can use the media center.

Use a Dictionary

You can look up *tiger* in a dictionary. Start by finding words that begin with the letter *t*. Then look for words that begin with the letters *ti*. Keep hunting until you find *tiger*.

Tt

table

A **table** is a piece of furniture with a flat top and four legs. Please put the jar on the **table.**

team

A **team** is a group of people who work or play together. Kim joined the soccer **team.**

telescope

A **telescope** is an instrument that makes faraway things look closer. Let's look at the moon through a **telescope.**

72

tiger

A **tiger** is a very large cat with orange fur and black stripes. Wild **tigers** live mainly in Asia.

toad

A **toad** is an animal that looks like a frog. **Toads** have dry skin and can jump long distances.

train

A **train** is a line of railroad cars pulled by an engine. **Trains** carry people and things.

73

Use the Library

Look for books that give facts about tigers.
Books that give facts are called nonfiction.
Storybooks are called fiction.

Tigers can live almost anywhere. All they need is food, water, and shade. They do not like to be out in the open.

Tiger cubs live with their mothers. When they grow up, tigers tend to travel alone.

34

35

Use the Media Center

You can use the classroom media center to find information. Use the Internet or a CD-ROM to look up facts about tigers.

Tigers

Where Tigers Live

What Tigers Eat

How Tigers Sound

Fun Tiger Facts

Questions

1. What should you do before you start your research?

2. Where can you look for answers?

Glossary

This glossary can help you to find out the meanings of words in this book that you may not know.

The words are listed in alphabetical order. There is a picture and a simple sentence for each word. You can use the picture and sentence to help you understand the meaning of each word.

Sample Entry

Main Entry   **Sample Sentence**

Plant

I love to **plant** seeds in the garden.

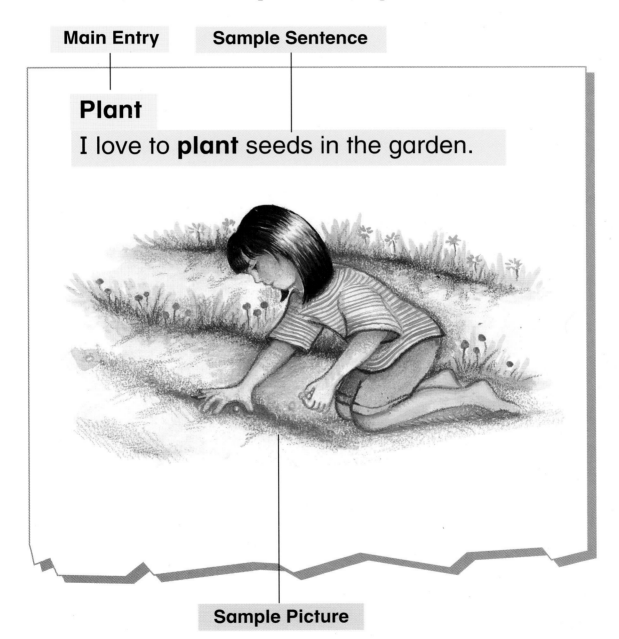

Sample Picture

Apple

An **apple** is a fruit.

Bag

Tim put the potatoes in the **bag**.

Another word for **bag** is *sack*.

Corn

I love to eat **corn** on the cob.

Ducks

Ducks are birds that swim in ponds.

Grapes

Grapes grow on a grapevine.

Hose

Water in the **hose** will help put out the fire.

144

Jars

The **jars** are filled with jelly.

Bottles is another word for **jars.**

Ladder

The **ladder** helps the fireman put out the fire.

Plant

I love to **plant** seeds in the garden.

Pole

The **pole** helps firefighters get to the fire quickly.

146

Rocket

The **rocket** travels to outer space.
Another word for **rocket** is *spaceship.*

Smoke

The **smoke** is coming from the burning
building.

ACKNOWLEDGMENTS

The publisher gratefully acknowledges permission to reprint the following copyrighted material:

"To the Top" by Sandra Liatsos. Copyright © 1992 by Sandra Liatsos. Used by premission of Marian Reiner for the author.

"Who Lived in a Shoe?" by Beatrix Potter from SING A SONG OF POPCORN. Copyright © 1988 by Scholastic Inc. Reprinted by permission of Scholastic Inc.

Illustration
Steve Johnson, Lou Francher, 6–7; Michele Noiset, 8–9; Shirley Beckes, 10–33, 34tl; Daniel Del Valle, 34br, 62br, 120b; Rita Lascaro, 35tr, 36, 64, 94, 122; Ken Bowser, 37, 123; Nancy Davis, 38–39; Dominic Catalano, 40–61, 62tl; Bernard Adnet, 65, 133; Doreen Gay–Kassel, 66–67; Tim Raglin, 68–93; Eldon Doty, 95; Kathleen O'Malley, 96–97; Michael Steirnagle, 98–119, 120tl; Darcia Labrosse, 124–125; Nancy Tobin, 132; Yuri Salzman, 134–5; George Thompson, 142; Peter Fasolino, 144–145; Holly Jones, 146–147.

Photography
40: b. Nick Cantalano/Courtesy of Dominic Catalano. 68: t. Courtesy of Ms. Ellen Dryer. 98: b. Courtesy of Michael Steirnagle. 143: b. Image Bank/Alvis Upitis. t. Corbis/Philip Gould; 144: t. The Stock Market/(c) Bo Zaunders. 145: b. Corbis/George Hall. 146: b. FPG international/(c) Ron Rovtar. 147: t. Image Bank.

READING FOR INFORMATION
All illustrations and photographs are by Macmillan/McGraw-Hill (MMH) except as noted below:
Photography
136 bl: MMH. 139: CMCD/Photo Disc.